Genetics

Genetics

Maureen Seaton

For more information on this book or to order, visit
www.jacklegpress.org

Published by JackLeg Press
Washington, DC

Second edition published 2021

First edition published 2012

ISBN: 978-1-7373307-5-2

Printed in the United States of America.

Library of Congress Cataloging-in-Publication Data

Cover design by Richard Every.

Also by Maureen Seaton

Undersea (2021)
Sweet World (2019)
Fisher (2018)
Tit, with Blue Guitar (chapbook) (2016)
Fibonacci Batman: New & Selected Poems 1991-2011 (2013)
Genetics (2012)
Cave of the Yellow Volkswagen (2009)
America Loves Carney (chapbook) (2009)
Sex Talks to Girls: A Memoir (2008)
Venus Examines Her Breast (2004)
Little Ice Age (2001)
Miss Molly Rockin' (chapbook) (1998)
Furious Cooking (1996)
The Sea among the Cupboards (1992)
Fear of Subways (1991)

Co-authored

Zero-Zero (chapbook, with Kristine Snodgrass) (2021)
Myth America: Poems in Collaboration (chapbook, with Carolina Hospital, Nicole Hospital-Medina, & Holly Iglesias) (2020)
Road to the Multiverse (chapbook, with Samuel Ace) (2020)
Caprice: Collected, Uncollected, and New Collaborations (with Denise Duhamel) (2015)
Madame Curie's Cookbook (chapbook, with Samuel Ace) (2013)
Two Thieves & a Liar (with Neil de la Flor & Kristine Snodgrass) (2012)
Sinéad O'Connor and Her Coat of a Thousand Bluebirds (with Neil de la Flor) (2011)
Stealth (with Samuel Ace) (2011)
Facial Geometry (chapbook, with Neil de la Flor & Kristine Snodgrass) (2006)

Little Novels (chapbook, with Denise Duhamel) (2002)
Oyl (chapbook, with Denise Duhamel) (2000)
Exquisite Politics (with Denise Duhamel) (1997)

Co-edited

Reading Queer: Poetry in a Time of Chaos (with Neil de la Flor) (2018)
Saints of Hysteria: A Half-Century of Collaborative American Poetry (with Denise Duhamel & David Trinidad) (2007)

Acknowledgments

2 Bridges Review: "Andy Goldsworthy," "Richard Grayson," "Ralph W. Emerson," "Saint Anthony and His Miracle of the Speaking Infant"

Adobe Walls: "Species," "When I Was a Speed Demon"

Another Chicago Magazine: "Prologue" [as "Genetics"]

Bathos Journal: "Found Liturgy (Redux)" [as "Found Liturgy 2"], "LA Dream #4 (The Devil)"

Blackbird: "Sex & Petroglyphs"

Bloom: "The Cradle of Life"

Chicago Review: "Revelation"

Colorado Review: "Sonnets for a Young Apostate"

Columbia Poetry Review: "Nasty Girls"

Diode: "Glinda"

Eckerd College Review: "LA Dream #5"

Fish Stories: "Physics"

The Gay and Lesbian Review Worldwide: "Sally Field," "Sex Talks with Girls"

Gulfstream: "The Asterina Motel"

Indiana Review: "An Ordinary Mass"

Jackleg: "Jump" [as "The Quantum Jump" from "The Great Quantum Mysteries"]

Mid-American Review: "A Nuclear Occurrence"

The Missouri Review: "Helplessly Hetero," "When I Was the Donna Reed Show," "When I Was the Virgin of Westchester"

New Letters: "The Bus of God," "Transliminal"

Pank: "When I Was Bi(nary)"

Paris Review: "Sing Sing"

Ploughshares: "The Church of God in Christ on the Hill"

Plume: "Ars Poetica, with Cow"

River Oak Review: "Envies," "The Strange" [as "Turn and Face the Strange"]

Salt Hill Journal: "St. Catherine of Siena Had Convulsions During Which She Radiated Light and Fragrance"

Sinister Wisdom: "Malcolm, Biting Upon My Left Ankle," "Queer Study (in Blue)," "Queer Study (in Red)"

Wisconsin Review: "When I Was Anorexic" [as "When I Was Thin"]

"Genetics" won an Illinois Arts Council Literary Award (with *ACM*).

"An Ordinary Mass" was reprinted in *Bless Me Father: Stories of Catholic Childhood* (Plume), Amber Coverdale Sumrall & Patricia Vecchione, eds.

"The Rogers Park Venus; Or, When I Was Sappho" was first printed in *The Zenith of Desire* (Crown), Gerry

Gomez Pearlberg, ed.; and reprinted with "Sally Field" in *Kissed by Venus*, "The Venus Salon," Jennifer Harris, ed.

"Noah Saterstrom and His Golden Armadillo" first appeared on http://www.noahsaterstrom.com, "Noah's Work-a-Day," and was written in honor of his "Golden Armadillo," drafted on November 28, 2010.

Infinite thanks to Emily Bowe, Jennifer Bowe, Lori Anderson, Sarah Gamoke, Linda Braasch, Connie Hough Cronin, Samuel Ace, Steve Butterman, Neil de la Flor, Denise Duhamel, Holly Iglesias, Marsha Keener, Mia Leonin, Niki Nolin, cin salach, Kristine Snodgrass, & Terese Svoboda. Finally, to Jennifer Harris, visionary extraordinaire!

For

Linda Braasch
Sarah Gamoke
Connie Hough Cronin

My Three Graces

Contents

Prologue

In my family we are mostly drunks. This is as cliché as moving to Chicago and everyone you know back home says: How's the Windy City? Or quarts of Bud and the New York Yankees. Or August at the Jersey shore. We all started out quirky in one way or another, uncles closing the bar at 3 AM, opening the church at 6, aunts taking to their beds, virgins everywhere.

A favorite story is the one about the sibling we mummy-wrapped for the Halloween parade at Edgemere Park—she was five or six and she looked really fabulous. Self-absorbed and morbid. A true ghoul. Still, she lost. Not even an honorable mention. Would not stop circling that baseball field. The judges finally went home. The best, scariest, ugliest, most demented. But that child walked around and around, stuck as a stick in a candy apple, until her big sister sat down on home plate and wept.

In addition to maudlin, we were all reputed to be quite wild. Mrs. O'Shea refused to let Kate go with me to the Straw Hat, but Kate was the one who got felt up in cars, not me. I just loved to dance. The wildness was something else, not the contagious kind, something inside, more like swinging out over the highway on a homemade rope or robbing houses in the neighborhood for no good reason. Praying not to wake up and then drinking enough to be truly blessed. Two sisters ate sleeping pills at different times, a brother was invited unceremoniously out of the service, we all flunked school. Then we straightened out. Not really.

It makes me think about genetics, what they'd do with families like mine, motorize us or colorize us or strain the bejesus right out of us. Stiff and brawly, all the daughters named some form of Mary, sons refusing to follow in the old man's steps. Would the world miss us? Would we trade our lives for ones of clone-shaped sanity? These are questions my family would never consider. These are questions that stray from the sorrow of all those parish events where we went seeking kingdoms and found boredom, where we waited for someone to come along and lift us from earth, but every time we looked in the eyes of the savior we saw ourselves, the line ahead of us, the line behind us reaching into a dozen different infinities, every one empty as the spaces in our DNA, where decisions fall and empires cast lots for the sculpting of a soul.

Pool of Saints

St. Catherine of Siena Had Convulsions During Which She Radiated Light and Fragrance

The flesh is untidy and hungry for discipline,
but I tried to hide all that. I was restless

for someone remarkable. I thought:
there she is in a child's hand, a field of flowers,

in blood. Every time I thought of her
I glowed, and once I plunged into a dark

and could not get back. At seven I reached
reason where there were darker smells,

how incense takes you from Good Friday
to the roof of the sanctuary with the martyrs

who flew around looking down on everyone
as if counting the lice on the living, yelling

at me to sing louder although my mouth,
as they could see, could not move. Sunlight

in the vestibule. Odor of young flesh
singed with the smallest flame. At twelve

I created a land on my left breast, etched
cities, disasters. I tasted my sibling's

phlegm, rolled it around in my mouth
like the first word until she was safe

inside me, one of four sisters
who slept like a wall against our father.

When I walked down the morning street
the citizens covered their eyes. Even before that

I had begun to cause my own light.
I looked at them busy with their lives

and they could not believe what they saw.
I was that bright, that drop-dead beautiful.

An Ordinary Mass

Everything holy seemed sad. Impossible karma,
wheels spinning death, resurrection, death,

ending in a garden of blood, Peter's ear on the ground,
all that betrayal. "The world is evil," the priest said,

so we waited for death to save us.

Things you find in heaven: Angels, of course,
in their wings and choir robes, each with perfect pitch.

Everyone in heaven is perfect, everyone's soul stainless,
you can put your hand right through people, they feel

prickly. The Apostles walk around on clean feet.
Women stand straight as trees. "The good

die young," said the priest, and "Satan loves a sinner,"
catching us between eternities of boredom

and brimstone. *Per omnia saecula saeculorum.*
Imagine the word: Forever.

The little red bells in my prayer book delight me.
Words that go with the bells take me from my body:

Elevate, sacred, adoration.

First we break the bones, then we devour him. Or
we break his bones, dip him in his blood, devour him.

Later we drink the blood. Sometimes the blood is red,
sometimes gold. When the altar boy rings the bells,

I feel Jesus enter my heart. There are no lasers yet,
but Mass is full of secrets and he gets into me.

I faint from kneeling up straight on an empty stomach.
Tucked in bed, I wait for the holes in my hands

to bloom like roses, the blood to run across the sheets
and change my life.

Sonnets for a Young Apostate

1

As a child, I thought about evil,
its basic forms and punishments, how
it leaves indelible marks on people—
tattoos and smirks on killers on death row,
my brother's fingers, stained and smelling
of unfiltered tobacco, age ten. While
I practiced a young Mozart, and the swelling
notes brought me great (nerdy) joy and wild
seasons of solitary guilt, *he*
wore black leather and broke into people's
houses in St. Anne's parish. We'd been taught
by the same teachers that stealing was evil,
that being good meant living life perfectly.
Luckily for us, we both got caught.

2

Luckily for us we both got caught
red-handed, so to speak, he with his
goods in the attic (how did he sneak them in,
what was he planning to do with them, what
dreams did they reveal?), and I, the older
sister with the boring A's and pheno-
barbitol for the courage to undergo
Catholic school with incipient ulcers.
He never opened a textbook, yet
grinned through graduation. I graduated
anorexic with a drug problem. We
polarized somewhere around thirteen,
he oblivious, I grief-stricken,
his life filled with risk, mine with religion.

3

His life filled with risk, mine with religion.
His friends had names like Cujo, while mine
spent long weekends retreating to convents
along the Hudson, obsessed with wine
becoming blood, bread flesh, and other
rituals of death and fear. Cujo
and my brother were cool as the leather
they hid behind. Arrested at school, Oh
Jesus, they sauntered, handcuffed and free,
to the local police car operated
by Patrolman Feeney with his German
shepherd wagging his tail behind him.
It was a sweltering day, my senior year.
I prayed Frank wouldn't smile, but he did.

4

I prayed Frank wouldn't smile, but he did,
and a part of me, his terrified, self-
appointed mother, cheered for the goof
of it all. Suddenly, without a hint
at how to be bad, I was notorious—
at least, related to notoriety
by blood. Hadn't we loved the same movies,
shared the same bunk beds for years? For us,
chocolate was bliss, green beans poison. Once
we'd slipped away from home to play on marble
headstones. We were Trigger and Lassie when
I fell and scarred my head for life: punishment
for having fun with Frank, which was what,
as a child, I thought about evil.

Sex Talks with Girls

When sleeping in the same bed with another girl, old or young, avoid 'snuggling up' close together...and, after going to bed, if you are sleeping alone or with others, just bear in mind that beds are sleeping places. When you go to bed, go to sleep just as quickly as you can. — J. D. Steinhardt, MD, *Ten Sex Talks to Girls* (1914)

1

Girls may appear innocent, even girls
whose breasts develop early and who
calmly wait for their body to grow hair
down there and under here, places no girl
should ever look. Turn your thoughts to creweled
coverlets. Cook a moist turkey, tat
a pillowcase. There is no better way
through puberty than the fine art of Home
Economics. Cupcakes are a great dis-
traction from awkward sexual urges.

2

Remember that God made Adam, and Eve
fell for a viper while our first man
stood by munching a Macintosh. Pity
boys—they aren't equipped to compete with snakes.
For instance, where would we be if Snow White
had settled for wildlife? Fairy tales are great
guides for living. Like *The Lives of the Saints.*
Saints had their hands cut off rather than sin.
Don't waste your time on girls. It's like kissing
a mirror or rubbing against a stuffed cat.

3

It is never okay to hug a girl
who looks like James Dean. If you're unable
to stop yourself, invoke the name of your
patron saint and think about martyrs. If
it's Joan, ask her to guide you through the fire
of your formative years. She herself died
too young to think about sex in her man-
ly clothes with her sword and her armor suit.
But remember: They burned her alive for her-
esy. (Even now, you've got to wonder.)

4

To summarize: Sleep quickly and alone.
Stay away from snakes, Joan of Arc, James Dean
flicks, and women's sports. Cook furiously
to appease hormones. Do not trust flowers.
Consider the seaside a possible
temptation. When developing a crush,
check for a *real* penis and stop yourself
if you don't see a white horse. Everything
should be Disney or saintly. Under no
circumstances should there be chemistry.

LA Dream #4 (The Devil)

A doorknob spins on the canvas of the dream. Closer and closer. Bigger and bigger. I never find this dream in any dreambook, no one can interpret a crazy dream like that. Next to my bed are my statues. I want more saints but I settle for Mary with her arms outstretched in blue robes. Nothing is impossible: Virgin, Mother. St. John Vianney opens the door to his confessional and there's Satan, which answers the question: Why did Vianney's hair turn white overnight?

If you've never been to the Monastery of the Precious Blood, don't go! The place is full of the goriest life-size Jesuses you've ever seen around every corner. This is where we have our freshman retreat and it's long after the doorknob dreams have stopped but devil dreams are worse. The devil will try to scare you if you're too good, so I sleep on the Castro Convertible outside my parents' room for months—I'm that holy.

Helplessly Hetero

Sally and her husband do not own a dog.
Karen and her husband exchanged vows just after her
brother and his wife.
Neither Lois nor Karen has children and neither is the
woman who is married to John.
Two couples chose paint the same color as their
carpets.

Karen and her husband exchanged vows just after her
brother and his wife.
The Carters, who own a bird, live in the apartment
directly below Kim and her husband (who isn't
Pete) and next door to George and his wife,
who have a pet named Twinkle.
Two couples chose paint the same color as their
carpets.
The Parrs do not have a sauna and do not live next
door to the Quincys.

The Carters, who own a bird, live in the apartment
directly below Kim and her husband (who isn't
Pete) and next door to George and his wife,
who have a pet named Twinkle.
The Whites chose the same color paint as the Browns'
carpet and the same color carpet as the Blacks'
paint.
The Parrs do not have a sauna and do not live next
door to the Quincys.
No couple chose carpet or paint the same color as that
described by their last name.

The Whites chose the same color paint as the Browns'
carpet and the same color carpet as the Blacks'
paint.
Amy and her husband have more children than the
couple LeAnn sat for on October 16th, but
fewer than Mark and his wife or the Browns.
No couple chose carpet or paint the same color as that
described by their last name.
Michelle is not Bob's wife.

Amy and her husband have more children than the
couple LeAnn sat for on October 16th, but
fewer than Mark and his wife or the Browns.
Neither Michelle nor Steve lives on Jay Street.
Michelle is not Bob's wife.
Tom and his wife, who aren't the Harrises, live on a
higher floor than Jim and his wife, who own a
pet named Chipper.

Neither Michelle nor Steve lives on Jay Street.
Neither Lois nor Karen has children and neither is the
woman who is married to John.
Tom and his wife, who aren't the Harrises, live on a
higher floor than Jim and his wife, who own a
pet named Chipper.
Sally and her husband do not own a dog.

(Note: All lines collaged from the logic problems of Mary A. Powell, Susan Zivich, Julie Spence, Diane Yoko, and Cheryl L. McLaughlin, *The Dell Book of Logic Problems #3*, 1988, Erica L. Rothstein, ed,)

LA Dream #5

I was Kathleen Turner plucked from her planned-out life and set down in my old car in the Bronx, heading the wrong way on Broadway, everybody beeping. Still, I was lovely with my honey hair and huge worry. I coasted down and away from something unclear. After a while I was no longer Kathleen Turner but someone with her DNA altered for survival. I ate berries. My hair grew down to my heels. I ended up in a kind of junkyard where I'd often gone in other dreams as other people, Maureen Seaton, perhaps. There were aspiring actors all claiming credit for my reentry into Universal Studios. They expected something in return so I said idleness had saved me. It's true, I said that, knowing they would say oh give me a break, and all I wanted was for someone to open the kitchen door and push me out.

Mapping

When I Was a Preteenybopper

I loved God first, then my (hip, boy) neighbor,
Jimmy H., who lived down the hill and smelled
like toast, as myself. It was second grade or

third when we first heard the Top 10 and held
pop summits in our bucolic backyards—
as the Milky Way spread its silver cold

incandescence overhead and our starved
young lives were mercifully fed by sound.
Our parents, young themselves, had harder

faiths, from crash or bomb or some wounded
core. Post-war, pre-funk, mid-Catholic, we were
naive lovers of bass, rhythm, spellbound

by something called a beat that could clobber
the righteous right out of us if we let it.
When those Billboarders crooned, my father

switched off their tunes and derided his
Little Darlin', Earth Angel, Sh-boom,
his derision no rival for cupid-

ity. His dogma dogged me until high school
when I fell in all the ways he'd foretold,
ways he'd threatened God would punish evil.

But when I was a bopper, radio
at my ear and all that soul inside me—
I was just a little fool for rock & roll.

When I Was The Virgin of Westchester

I spent every blessed dawn in the chapel
that beat on campus like a big cool heart
designed to extinguish sizzling coeds. Held

in myrrh, I hunkered in my pew, pet
dove to the angels both arch and anal
who hovered wholesome in white white white

and adorned me with lilies, then stifled
my urge to mouth and rip and tongue and bleed
with promises of wings and cloud wisps. Girl

yet woman, I esteemed the saints with their red
hearts blooming outside their blouses,
their celibate camaraderie with God.

"Sex!" my boyfriend said, and I was aroused
beyond my fear of boiling oil, my drear
religion crammed into crannies. Spouse

or not, I closed my eyes 'til I couldn't hear
the murmurings of Moses or the din
of Pope Paul VI or the solipsistic tears

of my guardian angels as I gave in
to my own Glorious Mysteries, bells
ringing sweet and spectacular with sin.

When I Was a Speed Demon

I raced my rocket, aerodynamic
and cunning, through traffic thick as ants
on watermelon. I was equipped

with the cerebellum of a hawk, stances
both swift and Don't Give a Damn all rolled
into one breathless quest for the chance

to fly across the finish line. Holy
Head Rush! and Who's With Me? I said to peers
with headlights, fans of spontaneity.

When I was fast, I was a girl with a queer
biology, brazen and muscle-y
yet kind of delicate, like a baby deer,

a fawn one day and antlered the next. Me:
caught between amphetamines and crinolines,
poser, puzzle, big teeter on a wee

totter, helmet with a ponytail. Win
or lose, I couldn't care less, I was daring
as Death and joined at the hip with his kin,

Velocity. I was unstrapped and wearing
thin lines between here and anywhere. Slick
and wheeling, I wiped out and poofed! mid-air.

When I Was Anorexic

I captured men in my Jones Beach bikini.
They were upside down in the stunted trees,
all possum and non-violence. My body

grew lucent and flumed daughters to cherish me.
My bones danced liquidly in loose muscle;
everything poked and burrowed. Heredity,

that gleaming defense, puffed up and wrestled
with numbers that shone like dreams come true,
that claimed I was spectacular. Held

this way, in grace and turpitude, I knew
new things. I waved in hallucination
and blood sugar. I behaved broth-ly: "Who,

me?" and "Why not?" Once I saw a scorpion
so small it fit beneath my tongue. Someone
lay beside me in adoration,

his eyes glazed as mine. His stratagem
swelled with tantra and hypocrisy
as we drifted toward cant and tedium,

until nothing remained of democracy
and my girl-cells, starved for estrogen,
trembled at the whine of autonomy.

When I Was the Donna Reed Show

I had an invincible routine. I cleaned
All Things That Shone on Monday: bathroom,
spouse. Tuesday I earned Household Saint for stain

removal. My soul gleamed behind the vacuum
Wednesday, traveled tip to top, stern to stem.
I grew rigorer and mortis. I crooned

like Electrolux electroshocked. Hemmed
and mended Thursday. Friday I shopped: Divine
Mother of A&P, grace-paced and amened,

round pearl face rapt in cellophane. Mine
was a clipped coupon of a winged week,
all bride and immolation, a fine

portrait of the house frau as an antique
doctrine, the drink the only way to make
right my robotic mysticism. Meek,

I switched to lush on Friday night, sleek
as a green silk sheath—*Pour me a Dewar's*—
then cracked open Saturday with a headache

the heft of Jupiter split into moons
and swinging scythes. It was Cold Duck, aspirin,
and mass on Sunday: God-holy truth.

When I Was Bi(nary)

I contrasted nicely with *unary*,
ternary, *quarternary*, and so on.
In this way, I functioned hypothetically

and trouble-free as a pair of bosons,
which, we know, will happily occupy
one quantum state, unlike two fermions.

Explosive, I fissioned and coded. My
planetary bodies orbited themselves
like a bi-asteroid, a bi-star (blue/white),

bi-nomials, and two cute daughter cells
that grew up opposite each other
and occasionally met in the middle

like lips. Sometimes I was a multiplier
in a two-based number system, enjoying
the way my human fingers desired

nothing more than the gratifying
mathematics of acey-deucey, ac/
dc, options flowing, always showing

off—like a superheroine or a tree.
For fun, I smote the rap of wishy-washy
and plucked the euphoric luck of binary.

Probability: Her Intrepid Divorce

Stage 1: In Which She Realizes She's Alone and Makes the Most of It

Ah, love, the first level of hell. And now Malcolm silks off the windowsill and pads my lap and kisses my forearm. He found me in the month of October—and, shit! I'm writing about my cat! Maybe I should turn to that lover, God, the way Dickinson did, or sing of me, but everything thou is me, even the bougainvillea calls on me to relate to it. I think that sky is there for me, I think the sea air sliding over my skin is mine alone and once (approaching non sequitur), digging a hole to the other side of the world, my brother and I accidentally bumped heads and lay unconscious through lunch time while our parents were in love with each other and vodka. Those days, if I hadn't been chubby, I would have been happy. I would have clung to the other kids around me, sandy and special with their peeling noses, and never let them grow up. If I can just think of life as being at a spa—that someday I'll be looking back at a woman who only had a short time alone before a new love walked through the door, and she used it well, stocking up for the two-timing ahead, the call to trust in someone besides herself.

Stage 2: In Which She Gives Advice to Her Unborn

It's good that I've got people close—the drunks and the tourists both—to keep me from growing backwards into a nun. I've set the place up almost, I've bought a drill and I'm ready to be a mother. All the babies look at me from heaven and want me, I can hear their feral hands swishing to grasp me yet I elude them saying: once you have fallen there is no going back, little one, no 360 degree return to the sun, you are forever touched by the body that brought you here and will carry it around less than jovially through all your future lives so watch out! And sure enough they stay cloud-bound and envious of red-faced infants who appear fulfilled. I am close to sky and beach here. Feel snuggled in this moldy motel. It's good it's all good it's all finally good. (It's 3 AM. She watches *Northern Exposure* in bed with her cat. Her uterus is a cradle, the seed of her first child rocking.)

Stage 3: In Which Her Denial Boils and Thickens

There are so many hushes there are the who and who of the black-ringed doves the intermittent puck puck of handball and guys yelling when they make points. The ocean is a block away and there's music. I can hear the guys yelling when they score and the music. There's a motel on the beach that echoes the ocean. When you walk by you hear the waves in stereo, a strange duet, and nothing is getting in tonight even birdsong leftover in ghosts and the yells and the puck puck puck. Sweet like this place in the night, sweet Friday. I'm surrounded on all sides by fictions but they don't appeal to me. I want this. The isolation and the extreme the precise and the solitary.

Stage 4: In Which She Reverts to an Extended Pirate Metaphor and Makes up a New Island

Tonight I was in the place of pirates again, perhaps the gold, always the gold tooth in the head of the swash and the buckle, the one meant to save me from boredom and lead me on to brimstone. It's the weather here: cold for February, fifty-eight in the shade and the sun keeps going away and there is a hush, there are hushes, even the neighborhood holds no music on a Saturday night. Florida. The Grand Dame. The Drug King. The Queen of the Atlantic. Here is my code coming into play, my pirate's code of ethics, take everything and give nothing back. If you can't swim, well then, sink. I was born on the opposite side of piracy, full of guilt and purity. It's a curse so I wait for the pirates to come along and swing from their ropes and carry me away to Sociopath Island in the middle of Who Cares. When I wake it will be without a worry, spilling priceless pineapple juice over the earth and letting it sink in without a thought, not recycling the box it came in, spitting in my lover's face if s/he fails to satisfy me—oh, pirate, I will say, you smell like rusty old doubloons from the bottom of the sea. You must wash before you steal me and never give me back.

Stage 5: In Which She Battles Paranoia

Perhaps the only way to measure the distance between the ocean and the intracoastal waterway is Marxism. Perhaps the man who lives across the patio is a mafioso. When he sees me in the morning he bellows my name and leaves again for "the airlines." I know he is no real pilot no flight attendant. Perhaps he runs drugs into South Florida from the tropics. Every week a package of "vitamins" appears at his door. (As long as no one kills him.)The French Canadian tourist in #1 suddenly thought he lived in my unit. I don't like that kind of mistake. I remember being really scared years ago when someone I knew married a man in prison and gave him my phone number. He would call me collect every day and I never once picked up—it was in the days of answering machines—but that didn't stop him from calling. He was looking for my friend who'd divorced him after he made a racist remark about the guy he'd murdered. She hated racists, she said. She said: Who could stay with a man after a comment like that? (*Argh.*)

Stage 6: In Which She Flies by Night

My stomach hurts from curried chicken and pancakes. I've havoc'd myself enough and need to walk but before that let me tell you what it's like in the quiet of Oscar Night, alone by the beach. I'll walk out there in a minute, but for now it's only the quiet and the puck of the ball on the paddle and little Bobby and his Mom and Dad doing laundry. Three people in two rooms and I am one person in four. It feels uneven. Like neighborhoods in Chicago that divide down the middle of a street with poor people on one side and yuppies on the other, usually along color lines, not always but usually, like a stop on the Ravenswood line—Sedgwick? My ex used to work for a guy on the rich side and she'd steal his stuff—quarters he left lying around, a little jewelry, some CDs. She thought he didn't know about it but years later he told her he knew. My theory is that he let her go ahead and steal his stuff out of guilt. Now there are railroad tracks between us, and a highway, she's on the west side, I'm on the east, flying by night.

Stage 7: In Which She Reaches a Rocky Acceptance

Several days ago I walked south on the boardwalk toward Miami. I listened to Canadians and watched as a woman jumped on her boyfriend's back and they both fell over and rolled on the ground, laughing. I poured my recycled cans and jars into a big blue bin and everyone waiting at the band shell applauded me for cleaning up the beach. They were drunk and funny and I was sober and depressed, tossing away my own seltzer bottles, hoorah! Malcolm accompanies me in this down time. Where I am he is, usually sleeping. But sometimes he meows at the door until I remind him that since we moved from the house to this motel he has a little pan of sand in the shower, not the whole outdoors to pee in. I keep thinking I hear the waves on the beach, but it's really just the wind in the sea grape trees. I'd love to write a poem, a real one with stanzas and enjambment. What would it be like to be dangerous enough for someone to want to assassinate? Or to be imprisoned for your beliefs? I ponder these questions until one day, many years later, I know the answers. In the meantime, there must be a place other than this one. I bet there's a portal to somewhere.

Sex (locus) Play

Two Episodes in Which Olive Ate the Spinach

1. "Never Kick a Woman" (1936)[1]

Take it easy, Skinny, you'll last longer, the Mae
West boxing instructor slurs to Mae Questel

(Olive's voice Oh!

Oh!). Then she punches our lanky lady into three
extreme hairstyles before Olive downs

the green stuff and crazy cat-fights West

to the (almost) death.

Olive sports Popeye's cap and smokes his pipe,
holds him tight and grins wide

for the cartoon camera—*toot toot.*

[1]http://www.youtube.com/watch?v=8VM8bvTkj-M

2. "Hillbilling and Coo-ing" (1956)[2]

A large lonesome hill*betty* steals Popeye from Olive and their blue roadster and threatens to *bill and coo* the sailor man into marriage, taking him *river smooching*. Popeye springs frantically to the top of an evergreen and Betty chops at it until Olive grabs the ax. *I'll teach you to chop down my Popeye*, says Olive, but Betty screws her at warp speed into a large tree stump. Meanwhile, Popeye accidentally drops the spinach and Olive sticks her tongue out about a foot and flips it into her own mouth while she's stuck in the tree stump, then swings Betty into space, where Betty chases the Man-in-the-Moon, who's not happy. Olive sings *I'll knock the dame sky-high who tries to take my guy*, and we see Popeye tied up in the trundle seat as he blows his pipe twice in relief and placidity. (*Toot toot.*)

2 http://www.youtube.com/watch?v=fxjui0IEwAo

Nasty Girls

(After *The Nasty Girl*, a film by Michael Verhoeven,1990, and on the occasion of Zora Neale Hurston's 100th birthday celebration, NYC, January 7, 1991.)

That celebrity's son's so hung up
on Zora's refusal to fit in
with the Renaissance, his
neck veins bulge big as snakes—
and I can't help but wonder tonight:
Am I nasty? Anna Rosmus
pissed off her Bavarian neighbors
when she uncovered Nazis in their clergy—
went from nice to nasty overnight!
And Zora Hurston's reputation as outlaw
followed her to Florida where
they laid her in an unmarked grave
and fed her books to the bonfire. Who
buried her, who burned her words,
who threw dynamite at Rosmus?
Am I nasty? Here's the folklore
of my people: They love their whiskey.
They count on salvation
at the end of purgatory,
attend Church and buy crullers
and crumb buns on the way home, and fat
newspapers, and Sunday is still
a day of gluttony and gossip.
I endangered my children once
when I gave up drinking and memory
caused a fury that overflowed.
I endangered them the day
I told them I loved a woman—

"No, honeys, listen to me, I *love* her."
And when their father took them away
to the house in Larchmont and the club
on the Sound I gave them to him
to save our lives, but I wonder:
Am I nasty? Is truth
worth such recklessness? Zora,
you're a hundred years old today.
From my room at the top of the city,
I honor you. From my freckles
and the blush that rises from my roots,
my raised-by-nuns will of iron,
I honor you, nasty girl, nasty
woman, nasty.

The Rogers Park Venus (Or When I Was Sappho)

She slides a disc into stereo
and lies beside her lover in a vast
breadth of futon on a curio

of a day in Rogers Park. She says this:
"What a curio of a day this is!" Love
responds with a sudden tumble of breasts

and sings in her deepest idiom of
cyclic device, symphonic flights in three
movements, a triple-spooned sonata.

Venus thinks Love's Cycles of Birth, Death, Re-
birth are zany. "I think you're really zany,"
she says but her lover has fallen asleep,

her mouth wide open, her bones and brain
relaxed as seaweed. Nothing quells desire
for her lover: twitch, drool, silly squished face.

Venus often says mythical things like:
For you I will burn the savory fat
of a white she-goat. This while she rides

the Cycle of Birth, that K2 high, that
sticky-fingers mango juice, that fresh cream
whipped in the middle of a thick moon night.

She is wrestling her lover's demons
to the ground. She is wearing her Cubs hat
backwards. She eats Twinkies. She says: *In dream*

we two were walking. It's not that she forgets
Lady Death during Love's sweet insanity
or that her lover's bones, translucent

as vacant oyster shells, don't constantly
remind her of the ineluctable depth
to follow. *I will sing beautifully*

and make you happy, dear comrade. It's as if
she holds all music inside her—breathy
sax and fevered flute, tongue of oboe, riff

of piccolo and slide guitar, slippery
harp. She says: "My love dreams in arpeggios.
Her *fire runs like a thief through my body.*"

Sing Sing

The day Jim stalks the tomcat between rows of bonsai,
I ask: What kind of gun is that? He says: Air.
And snuffs a squirrel as proof or demonstration.
At night we hear the turquoise neon terminator
frying bugs on the side lawn. Zap, scorch, shrivel, stick.
Lori moans in her sleep at the prolonged executions.
I have nightmares of fireflies betrayed by the mother ship.
Jim calls the female cat *slut* when she falls from grace,
bitch when she follows him on his walks in the garden.
Everything's beautiful here: gardenias, beefsteaks, lilies.
When we first moved in, our electric failed and Jim said
it was nothing but Com Ed's usual overpaid incompetence.
I imagine little chairs in the cellar wired for pesky pets.
Like living down the street from Sing Sing years back—
how our lights would dim and Grandfather say:
There goes another bum. And Mom would cross herself, we
kids stay angels for days.

Metropolis, Illinois

He's like Christ to my lover:
brave, ageless, secretly steel.

When she arrives at Best Inn
she asks first about the Klan—

therefore, she says, she can tell
by the way the clerk's eyes shift

if she'll still be alive by morning
or sent back to her girlfriend

in a body bag. *Don't*
let them bury me in a dress!

Her accomplice/homeboy,
Tom, plays Clark Kent to her

superhero. On him the gear
looks wannabe. On my lover

the hat fits perfectly, the boxers
like silk, and the tattoo above

her biceps says bighearted sex
with a bodyguard. This is a dream

fulfilled, this driving down Illinois,
straddling the South.

Whenever she lifts off
she looks back and expects

to find me calling *Superman.*
For all her daring, she's gone.

Queer Study (in Red)

Collage of Amy Lowell lines assembled
by Maureen Seaton

When I go away from you the world beats dead like
a slackened drum.

When I think of you, it is your hands,

A luster of crimson.

For I come at the times which suit me, morning or
evening, and I am cold when I come down the
long alleys to you.

But you—you come only as a harebell comes; one
day there is nothing, and the next your steepled
bells are all.

When you came you were like red wine and honey.

A thousand misconceptions may prevent our souls
from coming near enough to blend.

You would quiver like a shot-up spray of water.

I too should tremble, watching.

Queer Study (in Blue)

Collage of Maureen Seaton lines assembled by
Amy Lowell—as imagined by Maureen Seaton

She slips her finger in her mouth and walks me backward.
Her sweet clit and her blue jeans—
Orchids
Out of nowhere.
Blue then green then blue
Opals and quicksilver,
Reflection in cologne,
Dimples of Astroglide,
Lights pointing blue and cool,
Blue as jelly,
Blue-dress eyes.
The heart thrums between pubis and meridian—
Belly belly belly.
Oh transcendent, this aqua blue,
Divine fishes through blue.
She's gorgeous in her bones and blue.
The blue the blue the blue the blue the blue.

Sometimes Y

1 (Andy Goldsworthy)

I was born in the back of a baby blue Chevrolet with fins and a mom. My father caught me, then took me to the hospital surrounded by policemen. I was blue, then pink, then I was hunkered down and on with life. A year later my brother was born in a birthing bed. His hair was gold, his eyes green with kilts. At six I died (for six minutes precisely) and my brother grew invisible, like the back of a spoon. His little gold head became a wizard's head in the morning, a swan's egg at night. My father forgot him and my mother fed him sweet potatoes without looking. His name became Turtle, and when he grew up he built cairns and spires and long walls that wove silently through the glens of New York. They made a documentary about him starring Andy Goldsworthy. I watched it with my friend Steve, who looked at me and said, "Your brother Turtle is hot," and I was happy for Turtle then, for finally getting the attention he deserved.

2 (Richard Grayson)

The only way I might allow the accomplished healer Richard Grayson to enter me, and indeed the only way he might consider it, is through my sixth chakra. In this way he becomes a small triangle of indigo and extends himself outward and inward, a holisticist, mending my gray matter and my etheric brain at the same time. I would like to send him petals from my third eye, and if I have the opportunity, I will go to one of those trucks that park along the side roads by the beach in my town of Hollywood, Florida, and I will find an orchid for the honorable Richard Grayson, one for every time he ran for office and lost to anyone less worthy (everyone). In this way, I will stop the cycle of writing that has tortured me for the past twenty-five years and return to the fiction of my metalife before Richard Grayson, the hologram. I will write about myself in uncloaked terms, I will make up names that closely resemble the names of my family and a few ex-friends. Before I finish my life story I will appropriate memories from myself, and then I will tell everyone that, unlike his Holiness Richard Grayson, I am the great granddaughter to the tenth power of R.W. Emerson, and that when I die, I will join the Emersons at the banquet that awaits me in heaven. I will sit beside them, and they will try unsuccessfully to make me say grace.

3 (Ralph W. Emerson)

I shared lunch with a friend who wore a nice jacket and a striped tie, which might make one think the meal itself was a dressy meal, one that one would dress up for. Or, since my friend was the Head of English, the Chair of Grammar, I should say, rather, *one for which one would dress up. One for which an up kind of dressing would be appropriate.* To continue: I had my lunch backwards that day, typical of me under certain circumstances (funerals, ovulation), and when I went up to get my pudding first, I thought the word *desert* instead of *dessert* because that is a very common error in the English language which I particularly like to make, e.g. (for example), *the Mojave dessert* is a particular favorite of mine, as is *Would you care for some desert?* But I did not mention this to the friend I was having lunch with or with whom I was lunching, even though we both love a good faux pas almost as much as we love a chocolate moose.

4 (Saint Anthony & His Miracle of the Speaking Infant)

I'm sure there must have been some exceptional creatures in my life, a miraculous moment or two. My daughters walked early—does that count? Fat with grandiloquence, the infant in this old mural floats from woman to centurion to saint, who pixelates gracefully and leads me to believe that St. Anthony himself did not cause this miracle but has humbly witnessed it. He hands the baby to or takes the baby from the woman, who is not herself a saint (no telltale light), but tall and smiling, perhaps a mother at peace with her child's odd gift. The saint's head is bowed, his halo a ring of certitude, his ears a-blush. The centurion looks puzzled, a little lost, a little gay. I'm with him, baffled. My dog Poe was a perfect listener. Whenever I was sad as a kid, he made me feel better. Apart from Poe, I've never known a saint, at least not one who couldn't abide heretics as much as Anthony. Poe himself hated milk trucks. It was his job to chase them, and he did. One finally killed him.

5 (Gunga Din)

Whenever the siblings and our kids visited Pop in his final years, he'd sneak a well-worn video of *The Party* into his VCR cued to the scene where Peter Sellers, in offensive brown face and blood-stained turban as Gunga Din, dies comically of multiple gunshots while playing the bugle. My father's wife would take out her hearing aids and the rest of us would watch the short scene, laughing for the sake of our old man, who was, after all, mostly a good man. A decade earlier our mother had drifted downstream into her own dementia and had never come back. My father often dreamed she was not dead at all, that she'd hoaxed the whole thing and left him for the King of England. At the end of his dream, she'd float down a long flight of stairs with the King, holding his royal arm in a very alive way, and my father wondered if, instead of dying, she had merely divorced him. The day he turned 83, his makeshift wife stood beside him waiting for her hug, and before anyone could say *Gunga Din*, I wrapped my arms around her, picked her up, and threw her out the window.

6 (Noah Saterstrom & His Golden Armadillo)

Whenever I drive from Miami to New Mexico I count the dead armadillos along the way. One time, seven, another, eighteen, many of them babies, or at least teenagers. I've never seen an armadillo in any other setting, alive and sporting armor, so I was relieved to find this golden one snuggled up against a young man in Natchez, Mississippi, which is not on my normal cross-country route but now holds a definite appeal. What a great word: *Natchez*. The man has his arm around the armadillo and reclines in the middle of Main Street in a protective way, as if he knows armadillos are rarely alive after they've tried to cross a street or a superhighway. I can't imagine what it's like to touch an armadillo's back, which, they say, is leathery and has rough bands across it, preventing it from rolling up in a ball when threatened, as some might have heard. In fact, I can't believe it's true that the North American Nine-banded Armadillo jumps straight up in the air when surprised, and consequently collides with the undercarriage or fenders of passing vehicles. I'm glad this golden one has a friend. Plus, there's a huge eye looking down on Natchez. That should definitely help.

7 (A Baby Named Jamie, Hurt in December)

I met a baby recently who reminded me of a poem—in a slanted way, of course: the fractured lines, the blacks & blues, the internal keening. Then all the crazy loose threads weaving around like tentacles at the end of a calendar year started winding together and tying each other up, and I rode on my holiday armadillo through the wild and wooly holiday, lighting candles, faking faith, and heading toward the day a child's life would make some sense, when three men would find a baby beneath a star, place sweet herbs around his head, and fall in love with him on the spot. *Epiphany*, we say. A whole fucking sky of lights.

Evolutionary Theory

Revelation

So no one would dispute him, he said "historically"
empires have collapsed, folded, fallen, in other words

ceased to exist entirely at the precise moment
homosexuals walked openly in the public domain.

You mean (she said) that Gregg and Rick discussing
rings on Foster and Clark outside the Middle Eastern

store where we get great falafel are as powerful
as the Ice Age? That Val and Erica and Vanessa and Sue

gobbling plantains and curried goat and collard greens
and fried chicken at the Tropical Oasis near Lake

Michigan are a twentieth century equivalent
to the flood? They're Horsewomen of the Apocalypse,

four of the seven bowls of plagues?

His polemic went on logically (he hated Seuss) and soon
she was fitting her closet with bidet and microwave,

her dearest necessities, and he was driving
to Little Village for trysts with a masseur named Fred

whose working name was Las Manos, denying
that either of them was acting queerly. Off

they went disguised as straight to a disguised B&B
where couples took off their clothes and practiced

the cult of swinging, with others, for others, on others,
or around others, the option she chose because

she was unable to break free from the habit of
wholesomeness freckles automatically bequeath. Thus

time went on, she coveting girls, he coveting boys,
and on the seventh day they had a vision.

There they were on the Loyola Park Beach like Kiefer
Sutherland in *Flatliners* about to comment flatly and

irrevocably that indeed this is a good day to die when
they heard the sound of a ridiculous number of angels,

ten thousand times ten thousand...all living things
in creation—everything in the air, and on the ground,

and under the ground, and in the sea, crying.

And the animals said "Amen." And the elders from
Edgewater prostrated themselves on benches and slept

for decades as they longed to do. And they did.
It was the prelude to the prelude to the great day

that followed, when the seventh angel blew her trumpet
and the queers came out, every one, loud as childbirth,

and the world, as we knew it, died.

The Strange

Be mindful on those rain-spent days when litter pools around your toes and pigeons beckon. You'll be walking with your girlfriend in hetero-

steeped Harlem, NY, where the soul-food restaurant lady will pour salt on your collard greens like a layer of thin ice, your nice girlfriend

will produce a small knife and threaten several souls in the restaurant—you have a GIRLFRIEND, sweet Jesus, and while she's

navigating perfect sex with you behind bars that keep you trapped yet safe from the rest of New Yorkers, she couldn't possibly guess this is not

your true life. On the #3 home: not you. At Danny's Chicken: someone else. Driving the 18-foot Ryder with clutch and choke, the feet

that used to be yours don't even touch the floor—Jersey, Pennsylvania, Ohio, Indiana—ink-armed truckers signaling you to switch lanes

as if you belong. Be aware that on cloudless days of no obvious redemption, you'll be peddling books sincerely in the midst of a tornado watch,

cotton puffs blowing like snowy shrapnel around the Midwest sky, now you're IN THE MIDWEST, for God's sake, and no one knows this is not your normal life. Once you were snug between a father and a mother. You crossed your feet like a ballerina. On Halloween you dressed up

in a *Wonderloom* gown and a cap with a gold tassel. You had no idea how much a twelve-year-old could bleed, how empty you could become

in one rum-soaked night. There are days to watch out for—the non-charmed, the mammoth mundane—when the bells at Queen of Angels toll *Mary,*

we crown thee with blossoms and you wake beside a woman in Chicago.

A Nuclear Occurrence

There was perfect light and all the citizens walked back and forth with their shiny coats and their Midwest accents. I sat on the bench with my feet up reading Susan Griffin's *A Chorus of Stones*. Every time someone came close I felt nervous because I was reading frightening words—things the army does and things the government does, what happens to people who tell how dangerous it is, regardless of what my father said when he bought the place in Florida down the beach from the turkey vultures and the St. Lucie power plant.

Still the light was gold right before six and a couple strolled across the park with their chairs and their pencils and pads and different color skin and sat in the sun. One woman had on a cute straw hat. The other was bigger, bareheaded. I thought: Did the light on their skin exist before I came along to see it?

I'd observed turkey vultures once from a great distance, so when I drove by the St. Lucie plant and glimpsed a dozen of them standing by the side of the road, I naturally pulled over and grabbed my camera. I was smart enough to be cautious when security drove up, and I acted cool, remembering how harmless I tend to look, and sure enough, he wasn't too mad, just firm, asked me what I was doing and ordered me to leave. (This was a public road not five miles from my parents' house.)

It amazed me that the women in Chicago were so bold. Black and white, obviously a quote married couple unquote, right there in the biggest sunny clearing for all park-goers to see. They read and slept and sketched and talked like regular people while I kept my back to the tennis courts in case there was trouble.

On Hutchinson Island the vultures were congregating. Up close, their red heads looked pocked and disfigured. Circling above the highest trees they were spectacular. The day I observed them near the nuclear plant between the St. Lucie River and the Atlantic Ocean they were huddled and quiet. They commandeered the clearing and stared at me and the guard with his drawn gun. It was 1996. I was a schoolteacher with a camera. I caught them watching us from their world of peace.

The Church of God in Christ on the Hill

There's nothing more seductive than the basement
of this gated and clapboard building

in Bed-Stuy, Brooklyn, on a Sunday afternoon when
Sister Walker's got the turkey wings

and the fried chicken and the baked
macaroni and the green beans and candied yams

simmering on every burner in the tiny kitchen
while upstairs all the brothers sing

in witness, hallelujah, and the sisters jog around the church
because their knees don't have arthritis today

and their blood pressure is not up,
and the children sleep on soft cushions,

Sunday clothes pressed and red
and pink and Pastor's black robes flow

like the Nile with the baby Moses directly
to the arms of God. No one cares

Jesus and I are white. That I sit in my pew
one big blush of praise at the trumpets and the drums

and the tambourines in this Baptist orgy of the soul.
No one cares because THEY KNOW HOW TO WAIT.

"You can get by," Pastor Dallas says, "But, honey,
you can't get away." Talking about back-sliders,

talking about lapses of faith, infidelity,
homosexuality, God waiting patiently for revenge. I'm

thinking about the 'coon man out on the street
with those three dead-as-doornail raccoons

he climbed down the sewer to shoot last night
at the crest of his Bacardi high. I'm thinking

about Satan. And my Catholic upbringing
wafts around me like Sister Walker's chicken. As if

I've fasted since midnight, as if I'm eight years old
and Pastor says; "You have to make an *arrangement*

with God." Leaving out the g so I picture myself
arraigned before Jesus and Mary and the Twelve who

never had sex again after they heard the Good News.
Those raccoons laid out on the sidewalk

so quiet and guilty. Lori and I marching
toward the Church of God in Christ on the Hill

with our interracial fallen-away selves. As if
we're standing in the courtroom of God

and we're swaying from the turkey wings and yams
and Pastor Dallas yelling about the prodigal son,

how the father said: "Kill the fatted calf—
Don't eat that slop the pigs eat!"

And Lori says she's so hungry she could eat that slop,
and her grandmother says:

"Don't leave until after the altar call, girls."
But we do, walking down that aisle

as if we were holy. Those raccoons
baking in the sun on Rochester, 'coon man

drinking his first Sunday rum. All over
Bed-Stuy there's religion and sin,

homos and straight people, Pastor and 'coon man,
everyone getting mixed up in the witnessing

and the hunger and everyone
floating down the Nile toward the Pharaoh

or salvation.

The Bus of God

After Le Chat Lunatique

For Diane Larson, Muse and Master Sestinist

1

Usually (never) I'm traveling on the bus of God
with a whole band of violinists or crazy

bass players (5 string) who all whisper, *pssst*, then kiss
me before I can put up my (spit) guard, they're so tune-

ful, and skinny, those musicians. Such small teeth.
And pregnant all the time—like mermaids.

Kiss yourself (go on), I'll watch until you're all kissed
out and then I'll imagine I'm one of those mermaids

cutting fettuccine into boiling broth while tun-
ing out soulfully. Dear God,

the cellos are swallowing butterflies—they're crazy
in lower registers, right? Feet and crotch and molar.

2

Or graphic like the ones with or without photographs
of Superman. Oh. I can't feel my ears. I wonder what bruise

got stuck in there like a five-pointed star. I'm in the sugar
league, you know, a confection of wavy

particles and a commitment to the same old physics.
I sleep carefully, a nun named Joseph banging on the door
of my cell

or radio. I can't predict can you the simultaneity of waves
pretending to walk backwards through the sea that sleeps

between here and the Sargasso. Why don't you take a picture
why don't you. I'm blistering beneath this sugared

sun, all crisp and candy, I'm supposedly cell
deep in evolution, but every time I grow a hair I bruise

3

Far. I'm not a big fan of the way we all spelled Mississippi
as if it was the only childhood river, like

what was wrong with Chattahoochee, all those blues
and other vowels, and I like to think of our presidents

as rivers and our ex-presidents as stones,
but you won't catch me ever wanting to be one.

Whenever I see a river I think of all the presidents
who stood beside it and threw stones

sideways—skip and sink. Delaware, Mississippi,
bloodstreams, rivulets. All the water in Florida is blue.

All the water in Maryland is gray. Some of the water (one)
in New Mexico is brown. I like to walk on it.

4

Pretty soon I'll stitch myself to you—accost
me, go ahead, I dare you to spare

me just a little of your frequently flying female
(we're talking women here, right?). Wag on

my Sweet, go commando if you can't afford
a hat. I've got nothing against not going

and take off as if sleds and geese and wagons
could all get me to my dumb destination. A Ford

by any other name is a Chevy, my Tail Light, costing
about the same as a stunned or sequined mail

carrier. What? What? Are we ever going
to make sense of these tires of which this is a spare?

5

I've never had the kind of family that sucks fruit
or fingers, you know, the kind that drinks

gardenias. If you tell me Blythe Danner's
a water sign I could make you a pool to look at yourself in.

I can't seem to find the antidote to the fruity,
what do you call them, fractals, that open up

to reveal a stunning woman in boxers drinking
rosary beads or else that's an eel soaked

in the repetition of lemon juice. What bath
are we talking about? I'm still kind of sober

and looking for drinks that taste like Christ.
You call yourself a diorama?

6

Still, I could pretend I'm blue, like a blurted orgasm, name
myself a heteronym that rhymes with power or hang her

or check again when she's dead and out of luck(y)
pennies, my sweet nasally girl, my little tiny petit

four-three-two, my sugar lump, mine, mine mine—
sometimes I am so baffled I can only (it's not my fault) read.

Or she is also alas anon a leery loud and lucky
persimmon of purse string theory. Why is everything red

when you want it to be more subdued-ish, a little
more like the whispered cagey name

of an aging hooker, not a screamer, more a hanger
on like a sheep inside a box or a woman inside a gold mine.

7

You are a fault line, a scarab, a drool.
I am your figure of speech, oh Lynchmob, oh Fab Face.

Come a come a come a come a come come a come a.
You are my spinal tapper, my scrunchy pearls.

I am your, let's face it, boomerang.
And you have earned me, learned me, burned [okay, me].

And now all I can think of is: what kind of gem
should I serve at a breakfast of meaningful

clergy? I could hope for the same sundial
you poked inside me during the member-

ship drive, or I could rely on Einstein
or Frankenstein, and simply marry you.

Envies

The last extraordinary thing about you
is your noise and I've wanted that too, the way
your throat opens when you laugh and lets out
animals, the way everyone listens
because you sound so tall. Your irreverence
in the face of order and law makes me
want you to slip like a double inside me
and make my eyes inch along a woman's
body the way yours do, my hands move
across her shoulders and follow her spine
to the well, that place where a small spilled glass
of wine pools without movement on her part.
She's so still lying there waiting for your tongue
on the wine. She almost looks like me.

Physics

I hold an atom in my hand
and it's silent as thought. Or I move

and the atom spins fast—
it's big and little, breaking apart.

My lover runs toward the third rail,
detonation like a comet in the bedroom,

glass in the eye, waves and particles
exploding. If I had a son I'd

name him after her.
There he is at the controls until

his fingers fall off and he's eaten
every bit he could stuff in his mouth.

So big its nucleus is an enormous dome
with a speck of dust around it.

So little we can't see it without
causing it to flinch and even then

we can't see it in a million years.
People leaving people drives me crazy

as Jesus on the cross saying *Today*
I will see you in paradise to only one thief.

Transliminal

Sometimes my heart is rocking my body, I can feel it like a train beyond the prairie rattling West and I wonder where it leads or if the time it takes to say *I believe* is enough. All the perturbations of a life, the fine rippling silt in the bottom of the little river.

The ultimate level of significance is especially highlighted in moments of transition: one consciousness to another. (Robert S. Ellwood)

Every 15 years the person I'm currently married to goes out and sleeps with someone else. I picture these women as blond and crass, I can't help it, although I know only one was blond, the other gray. And only one was truly crass.

I picture them a little desperate, a little hopeful, but mostly I picture them thinking: *innocence, opportunity.* In both cases my spouses believed they'd been treated unfairly, but they were both Leos and therefore, I've learned since, completely incapable of introspection. The first time it happened I put my mouth into the living room carpet so I wouldn't wake the kids. This time the kids were grown.

Nietzsche said every age has a limit or horizon that can be seen as horizon only when it has been transcended.

An age may be nothing but a particular conversation, a fall from a bridge.

I miss my mother-in-law; I called her Mommy because she felt like one even though she was only fourteen years older and very beautiful. I notice people either treat me with great kindness or great cruelty, as if I were a child. In the six years I knew her we gave each other the benefit of the doubt many times. I like the benefit of the doubt. It means you think the best of a person even when you don't understand exactly what she's trying to do and it may seem at first not such a wise or a good thing.

Still the whole idea of infidelity disturbs me, like that anecdote of putting a puzzle of the world together then turning it over to find the family on the other side. And vice versa.

Today I went down to the suspension bridge where my friends jumped so hard I was afraid it would break. It didn't, but how could I have known it wouldn't, they jumped so long I figured it had to. I guess I'm not the type to jump merrily on a puny bridge that hundreds of people will have to cross sometime in the future.

My puzzle's got strange women on the back from Portland and Miami, two places I've never been. And once, when we were kids, my brother fell headfirst into the river. He was wet, I was dry. We were running toward home, we were trading our clothes between horizons.

Drift

The Asterina Motel

It's the powerful granddaddy time when all you have to do is wish on a manatee and it will be done.

I wish on the wind and the plummeting pelicans.

Malcolm sleeps with his paw on the caps button. He dreams of lizards and his former freedom. At night I wake to hear him running around my bed, a gigantic seahorse.

Two humans snorkel. Their gaze holds the starfish in place as if she were pinned to the sandy bottom, as if she were so special they can't resist reaching down and bruising her.

I meet a woman with enormous tattooed wings on her back. *Look at that ocean*—she says, proudly—*like a lake!*

My old landlord would arrive with his SUV full of Bud and a raft of tools to share with his cheap labor. They'd mix cement for weeks—a sound like chewing inside your head—they'd frame and fashion—wood on concrete on wood—forming the way up from the ground floor to the second. Once they drilled right through a water pipe.

Ceci n'est pas une pipe! they must have thought.

Now I'm caught between grief and mockingbirds.

There are doubloons in this sand still stained with blood and three granddaddy manatee heading north, barely visible in the sea.

My wishes will come true when they come up for air.

Sally Field

If I could be any actor it would be Sally Field. If I could sleep with any actor it would be Queen Latifah. Field reminds me a little of me if I weren't so phobic about flying.

Latifah, you might say, has become a famous femme in recent years—if you judge by the makeup and the glossy magazine spreads. Still, the way she rapped

in the old days…and that *Set It Off* scene. The thing I like about Field is her seamless approach to her life and work. Plus she's a mom and she says censorable

things. I like that she loved two men in *Norma Rae*. I've had trouble myself loving just one person over the years. I could easily have three lovers at a time like a Mormon

or a beach cat. Queen Latifah reminds me of the night one of my lovers dressed up as a femme fatale and sang me a torch song. Not all butches can do that. Some look like drag queens

when they put on femme clothes. Even with a construction hat and steel-toed boots I femme myself out. That's where Sally Field and I have something else in common.

Cowboy boots just make us look cuter.

Glinda

I've often picked web-footed partners or sibilant ones who required special hearing on my part. A Doctor in a Petri dish. A Dairy King.

The cause of my attraction has been unpremeditated and dangerous, like sodium, or magnified to many degrees of powerlessness, like Poncho Villa.

The replications I've squandered resemble my old almost high school sweetheart, John Q. Meany. Before I turned so gay.

Often it was just someone playing with wigs or the idea of wigs, throwing a wig party or, later, being in the mood for wig-like collaboration.

Before that there were some I chose and others I thought looked too much like pudding. I couldn't wrestle them all, not in this getup.

Sex & Petroglyphs

Once, when the volcanoes threw ash too far and the people had carved the cold, it was war happening backwards. You petrified me with your funny little hat and your short skirt. Sometimes I'd come home and there'd be nothing on TV. Those were dark times made of bones and litigation. Of phenominalism (the theory that all existence is calcified and litigious). From there you plucked the space between ethics, a wicked sticky clench of a place never before explored or expunged, although we both expatriated. You can see where I'm going with this. I wasn't supposed to notice the way everyone in the stained glass turned to look at me. I began to think: I could. I could actually marry a priest. Or a pirate. Don't say the ways we kill and heal each other crawl around like sex inside us. Say: I am soon to appear before you with a golden crown.

Species

1

The girl who kissed the fish sits over there ordering a Buddha Bowl from the guy who makes them who must be her boyfriend and who obviously (you can tell by his blasé blasé) does not know she has just kissed a fish. Look at her, all ocean. Do you know what I mean, Dovey? Like owning land—what is that? I'm off the point. Fish kissing is fun. I did it once near the Atlantic. Behind a neighbor's sunken ship, my turquoise gills glistening.

2

What is most crucial is the answer I hear when I'm not asking anything. Hey, there's a coot. Bring everything you've ever desired to the windows that wrap around our glowing lives. Yesterday I joined a gym in Albuquerque. A real one, with executives bicycling on their lunch hour and women ignoring each other in the locker room. It scared me. The way I used to be scared when I thought about heaven—how I'd be there forever someday. An incomprehensible loop, an etymology of nothing. We're such grounded creatures, my Piñon, my Little Seed of Dreams.

3

And suddenly she was a mallard, a male with an emerald head. She had a wife with ducklings on the way and a long yellow beak to scoop the water for bugs. She wished she was that turtle on those logs, still and resting, looking like the logs, waiting for something amphibian to happen, polliwogs or newts. Whenever she tried to think, it was only water, water, water. Her feet flashed like fins. Her feathers were oily and nothing they did reminded her of her old head of hair when she was a woman with a husband of her own sitting in front of a pond looking at ducks. Ducks are so beautiful, she used to think, and then she observed herself realize she would never be able to eat one again.

Ars Poetica, with Cow

What is so innocent as grazing cattle?
If you think about it, it turns into words.
—from "Always on the Train," Ruth Stone

She went back to look at the cow, which lay immobile except for one eye watching the girl who stood helpless beside the ditch. It soon snowed, and in the spring the cow was a perfect frozen corpse of cow, cradled in the ditch like an exhibit. The girl visited her until the cow was nothing more than bones and hide, and even then, a warm heart pumped between them.

It was easy to love the girl if you were a cow in the middle of an enormous field in a state three times the size of Ireland. Otherwise, the girl was thought strange, as many throughout time have been thought strange. She was like a tree that laughs into new centuries. In this way she defied the odds, being odd herself and brave beside the dying and the dead.

In the years that followed, as she launched herself from the tops of aspens and cottonwoods, it was the way she called herself back, that spot of field, that rite of recognition. I'm here, she would say, landing in warm shit beside rattlers and pine beetles, on buttes and precipices, and the words carried across freezing fields into the minds of cows and made her life and theirs indistinguishable.

Malcolm Biting Upon My Left Ankle

After Amy Lowell's "Still Life, Moonlight
Striking Upon a Chess Board"

I am so aching to write
That I could pull a mitre from the space-time continuum
And stick it, cockeyed, on the head of my wicked cat
And make him alive again and Pope.
He might have been a king, but he lacked cupidity;
He might have been a purebred, but where is the
    fun in brushing and posing.
Malcolm, our affinity is rare and canonical,
For I, too, am all ouch and deconstruction
Perpetually biting you back, you green-eyed god.

Jump

The electron is caught inside a black hole. Oops, there it is outside the hole—no discernible path. Neither have we ourselves been able to free it in any way. This is how some of us recover from a great shock. One day we can't see shit, the next we're outside the hole. We don't understand. We don't have to. It's impossible not to want to thank something, however, and for this we created God. Thank you, we say, those of us who have leapt crazily without any thought to our limitations, without any conscious hope at all. God or luck. God, luck, or fate. God, luck, fate, hard work. God, luck, fate, hard work, genetics. Pick one. Every time, you will be wrong.

Found Liturgy (Redux)

If I'd married the gentle man with the crooked lip instead
of the vicarious bohemian with a propensity

for large butts and rosy knee caps, I'd have strolled along in
sublime serenity, not rumbled through my

maiden phase like the Howard bearing down on North and
Clybourn, that turn in the tracks where

the conductor says *Whee* and we're expected,
faithful congregation, to lean left and continue

whatever religious rites we practice on subways: prayer
beads, bible, clawing, dreaming.

One day I might have departed for a bluer, warmer place,
moved away from this country altogether,

to Mojácar, Spain, with its women who laugh (ha!) at the
scrawny models in *Cosmopolitan* while their

men recall the sweet fucking of the night before.
Even the thought—goofy, apocryphal—that had I

chosen which body I'd prefer to inhabit as I waited on the
cusp of the universe, I'd have chosen

soprano, green thumb, old wealth, rock star.
The thought that someday we will all live together

on the head of a pin or fly to the uninhabitable moons of
Jupiter to experience options

of antioxidants and uninhibited youth. Everything I've ever
thought I *had* to think, think of it, every

synapse, every charged neuron tingling along its DNA,
every scarlet image, every note I've plucked

in *A* or *D* or *B*: preordained as the teetering
ascendancy of America. I love the word *kismet.*

I love throwing it into the atmosphere to see what it brings
back. Once it brought back a woman who

landed in my lap in the key of *G*, a key I instantly
recognized and sang: *Melancholy Baby, Sweet Adeline*,

O Holy Holy Night.

The Cradle of Life

(Letters to my daughter)

It's only what drives you more and more
openly to suicide that saves you.
—Walter Lowenfels,
Letters to an Imaginary Daughter

I took Lori to see *Lara Croft* for her birthday today and my favorite part was when Angelina flew in her parachute outfit and landed feet first on a small boat. Outside the theater was a makeshift barnyard in honor of another movie, *Seabiscuit*, which made little sense since there were no horses present. I couldn't watch the kids poke the goats and ducks, so Lori took me home and here we are, waiting for the drawbridge on Dania Beach Boulevard. Lori turned 49 today and said she wants to have her 50th birthday in Far Rockaway at her mother's house, and I got really sad because I'll be leaving Lori before she turns fifty, although she doesn't know this yet and neither do I.

Before the movie I saw a woman on the ticket line who lives down the street from us. She walks to the beach every day, stays there a long time with her friends, then walks back to her condo. She has very short hair and is thin, the way I would like to be, but instead I get to sit and write poems. That's my theory. She smiled and waved to me, something she'd never done before. If I had a beautiful body, which I did for exactly three months once when you were eight years old, I might be a bathing beauty too. Not that I don't like using my mind. It's a good consolation prize. But when I chose which I wanted more, good body or brain, I don't think I was properly informed about where I would be living one day or who my neighbors would be. You can tell I kind of rushed through the orientation, grabbing cookies as I headed for door #2.

Last week someone died in a jet-ski accident, and I thought of that today during *Lara Croft* because Angelina Jolie and her double were showing off on a jet-ski. When I was a musician, I used to worry about my hands, what I would do if I ever lost or injured them, plus, how would I type? Which is what I'm doing right now, typing some crazy stuff in Florida as you do the same a thousand miles away in Chicago. Malcolm just meowed until I yelled at Lori to feed him—not yelled yelled, just loudly through the back door so she could hear me. She's 49! By all rights, having had her arm almost completely severed one time and having fallen halfway through two moving subway cars another, she should be dead. Yet here she is, nodding in the heat and waiting for Chinese food, which is what she wants for her birthday celebration. I offered to take her out anywhere, but I think she was influenced by the movie, which took place partly in Shanghai. She leaned over, whispered, *Where's Shanghai?*

Now there's a scuba diver in the turquoise part of the sea. He's underwater, searching for the Cradle of Life. I read that it's hotter in Chicago in July than it is in Miami, and since I've lived in both places I know this to be true. The other day I got seasick from floating on my back in a totally calm sea. I've gotten seasick in the backs of cars, on airplanes, on waterbeds, and in a flotation tank in Chicago that was meant to reduce sensation, bring me to my higher self. Apparently, my higher self needs Dramamine. The temperature of the sea in Miami is as high as the air—87 degrees. In Chicago, Lake Michigan only makes it to 65.

I forgot to say that the average high for July in Chicago is 95 degrees and the high for Miami in July is 92 degrees. It gets hotter in Chicago in July but not for very long. Remember the year several died in the heat up there? *Melters.* They say that people make jokes to feel better. When Lori and I went to the Everglades we took a boat tour and hit a huge electrical storm. Lori sang the theme from *Gilligan's Island.* Everyone laughed. She herself laughs at every opportunity. I've seen people cross over into hysteria around Lori quite easily. I keep telling her she could do stand-up or run for office. The Cradle of Life mostly exists in movies and books, although I got close to it once in Wyoming. The scuba diver is gone now, his little yellow flag no longer bobbing up and down. He must have left the sea while I wasn't looking. Like the day there were three manatees heading north about a hundred yards out and I had my back to the ocean, working on my tan. That day my thin neighbor and her friends ignored me as usual and Lori was asleep back at the house. Some guy tapped me on the shoulder and said: If I were you, I'd turn around.

About the Author

Maureen Seaton has authored twenty-two poetry collections, both solo and collaborative—most recently, *Undersea* (JaackLeg Press, 2021) and *Sweet World* (CavanKerry, 2019), winner of the Florida Book Award in Poetry, and the chapbooks *Myth America* (Anhinga, 2020), co-written with Carolina Hospital, Nicole Hospital-Medina, and Holly Iglesias, and *Zero-Zero* (Hysterical Books, 2021), co-written with Kristine Snodgrass. Her honors include the NEA, Pushcart, and Lambda Literary Awards for *Furious Cooking* (Iowa, 1996) and *Sex Talks to Girls: A Memoir* (U. of Wisconsin, 2008, 2018). Her work has appeared in *Best American Poetry* and numerous anthologies and literary journals. Seaton is Professor of Creative Writing at the University of Miami and was voted Miami's Best Poet 2020 by The Miami New Times.

Titles

Back Apart, Barbara Cully

Under the Hours. Barbara Cully

Hallucinogenesis. D.C. Gonzales-Prieto

Trapline. Caroline Goodwin

This is How I Dream It. Jennifer Harris

Men in Correspondence. Meagan Lehr

Observations of an Orchestrated Catastrophe. Jenny Magnus

when i am yes. cin salach

Two Thieves and a Liar. Neil de la Flor, Maureen Seaton, and Kristine Snodgrass

Genetics. Maureen Seaton

Undersea. Maureen Seaton

The War on Pants. Kristine Snodgrass

jacklegpress.org

www.ingramcontent.com/pod-product-compliance
Ingram Content Group UK Ltd.
Pitfield, Milton Keynes, MK11 3LW, UK
UKHW041640190726
13854UKWH00006B/2606